Westminster Shorter Catechism

Thank you for choosing to use these copywork pages with your child. Each of the following pages is a question and answer from the Westminster Shorter Catechism (WSC). There are 107 questions in the WSC and 111 pages of copywork (a few of the answers were too long to fit onto one page). This copywork (labeled I for intermediate) is ideal for a student who is comfortable with writing and does not need guidance in letter placement. The words are placed directly above each line and the lines are approximately the size of the lines on wide-ruled paper.

These pages would be a perfect complement to any child's study of the 17th century, the Bible, or English history. The questions and answers will be thought provoking, challenging, and beneficial for your student. This copywork pack would be especially helpful if your child is planning on memorizing the WSC. Please note that the original language has been preserved so there are some accounts of Old English words like 'doth.'

Copywork is a fantastic way to help your child master reading, penmanship, grammar, and spelling all at the same time, simply and subtly. I hope you and your child enjoy using this copywork pack together!

Amy @ www.classicalcopywork.com

Westminster Shorter Catechism

Copyright © 2013 by Amy Maze

Published by Classical Copywork – www.classicalcopywork.com

All Rights Reserved. These pages may not be:

- Modified in any way (including removing the copyright or any other proprietary notations)
- Copied (except for use within your immediate family)
- Used for commercial purpose or public display
- Shared with others (please direct people to the website so they can download the pages themselves)

Westminster Shorter Catechism

> Question 1. What is the chief end of man?

Man's chief end is to glorify God, and
_____
_____
to enjoy him forever.
_____
_____

Westminster Shorter Catechism

Question 2. What rule hath God given to direct us how we may glorify and enjoy him?

The Word of God, which is contained

in the Scriptures of the Old and New

Testaments, is the only rule to direct us

how we may glorify and enjoy him.

Westminster Shorter Catechism

Question 3. What do the Scriptures principally teach?

The Scriptures principally teach what

man is to believe concerning God, and

what duty God requires of man.

Westminster Shorter Catechism

Question 4. What is God?

God is a Spirit, infinite, eternal, and

unchangeable in his being, wisdom,

power, holiness, justice, goodness, and

truth.

Westminster Shorter Catechism

> Question 5. Are there more gods than one?

There is but one only, the living and

true God.

Westminster Shorter Catechism

Question 6. How many persons are there in the Godhead?

There are three persons in the Godhead; the Father, the Son, and the Holy Ghost; and these three are one God, the same in substance, equal in power and glory.

Westminster Shorter Catechism

Question 7. What are the decrees of God?

The decrees of God are, his eternal purpose, according to the council of his will, whereby, for his own glory, he hath foreordained whatsoever comes to pass.

Westminster Shorter Catechism

> Question 8. How doth God execute his decrees?

God executeth his decrees in the

works of creation and providence.

Westminster Shorter Catechism

Question 9. What is the work of creation?

The work of creation is, God's making all things of nothing, by the word of his power, in the space of six days, and all very good.

Westminster Shorter Catechism

Question 10. How did God create man?

God created man male and female,

after his own image, in knowledge,

righteousness, and holiness, with

dominion over the creatures.

Westminster Shorter Catechism

Question 11. What are God's works of providence?

God's works of providence are, his

most holy, wise, and powerful

preserving and governing all his

creatures, and all their actions.

Westminster Shorter Catechism

Question 12. What special act of providence did God exercise toward man in the estate wherein he was created?

When God had created man, he

entered into a covenant of life with

him, upon condition of perfect

obedience; forbidding him to eat of

the tree of the knowledge of good

and evil, upon pain of death.

Westminster Shorter Catechism

> Question 13. Did our first parents continue in the estate wherein they were created?

Our first parents, being left to the freedom of their own will, fell from the estate wherein they were created, by sinning against God.

Westminster Shorter Catechism

> Question 14. What is sin?

Sin is any want of conformity unto, or

transgression of, the law of God.

Westminster Shorter Catechism

Question 15. What was the sin whereby out first parents fell from the estate wherein they were created?

The sin whereby our first parents fell

from the estate wherein they were

created, was their eating the

forbidden fruit.

Westminster Shorter Catechism

Question 16. Did all mankind fall in Adam's first transgression?

The covenant being made with Adam not only for himself, but for his posterity; all mankind, descending from him by ordinary generation, sinned in him, and fell with him, in his first transgression.

Westminster Shorter Catechism

> **Question 17. Into what estate did the fall bring mankind?**

The fall brought mankind into an estate of sin and misery.

Westminster Shorter Catechism

Question 18. Wherein consists the sinfulness of that estate whereinto man fell?

The sinfulness of that estate whereinto

man fell, consists in the guilt of

Adam's first sin, the want of original

righteousness, and the corruption of his

whole nature, which is commonly called

original sin; together with all actual

transgressions which proceed from it.

Westminster Shorter Catechism

> **Question 19.** What is the misery of that estate whereinto man fell?

All mankind by their fall lost

communion with God, are under his

wrath and curse, and so made liable

to all miseries in this life, to death

itself, and to the pains of hell forever.

Westminster Shorter Catechism

Question 20. Did God leave all mankind to perish in the estate of sin and misery?

God having, out of his mere good

pleasure, from all eternity, elected

some to everlasting life, did enter into

a covenant of grace, to deliver them

out of the estate of sin and misery,

and to bring them into an estate of

salvation by a Redeemer.

Westminster Shorter Catechism

Question 21. Who is the Redeemer of God's elect?

The only Redeemer of God's elect is

the Lord Jesus Christ, who, being the

eternal Son of God, became man

and so was, and continueth to be,

God and man in two distinct natures,

and one person, forever.

Westminster Shorter Catechism

Question 22. How did Christ, being the Son of God, become man?

Christ, the Son of God, became man, by taking to himself a true body, and a reasonable soul, being conceived by the power of the Holy Ghost, in the womb of the virgin Mary, and born of her yet without sin.

Westminster Shorter Catechism

Question 23. What offices doth Christ execute as our Redeemer?

Christ, as our Redeemer, executeth the offices of a prophet, of a priest, and of a king, both in his estate of humiliation and exaltation.

Westminster Shorter Catechism

Question 24. How doth Christ execute the office of a prophet?

Christ executeth the office of a prophet, in revealing to us, by his Word and Spirit, the will of God for our salvation.

Westminster Shorter Catechism

Question 25. How doth Christ execute the office of a priest?

Christ executeth the office of a priest, in his once offering up of himself a sacrifice to satisfy divine justice, and reconcile us to God; and in making continual intercession for us.

Westminster Shorter Catechism

Question 26. How doth Christ execute the office of a king?

Christ executeth the office of a king, in subduing us to himself, in ruling and defending us, and in restraining and conquering all his and our enemies.

Westminster Shorter Catechism

Question 27. Wherein did Christ's humiliation consist?

Christ's humiliation consisted in his being born, and that in a low condition, made under the law, undergoing the miseries of this life, the wrath of God, and the cursed death of the cross; in being buried, and continuing under the power of death for a time.

Westminster Shorter Catechism

Question 28. Wherein consisteth Christ's exaltation?

Christ's exaltation consisteth in his rising again from the dead on the third day, in ascending up into heaven, in sitting at the right hand of God the Father, and in coming to judge the world at the last day.

Westminster Shorter Catechism

Question 29. How are made partakers of the redemption purchased by Christ?

We are made partakers of the redemption purchased by Christ, by the effectual application of it to us by his Holy Spirit.

Westminster Shorter Catechism

Question 30. How doth the Spirit apply to us the redemption purchased by Christ?

The Spirit applieth to us the redemption purchased by Christ, by working faith in us, and thereby uniting us to Christ in our effectual calling.

Westminster Shorter Catechism

Question 31. What is effectual calling?

Effectual calling is the work of God's

Spirit, whereby, convincing us of our

sin and misery, enlightening our minds

in the knowledge of Christ, and

renewing our wills, he doth persuade

and enable us to embrace Jesus

Christ, freely offered to us in the gospel.

Westminster Shorter Catechism

Question 32. What benefits do they that are effectually called partake of in this life?

They that are effectually called do in this life partake of justification, adoption, and sanctification, and the several benefits which in this life do either accompany or flow from them.

Westminster Shorter Catechism

Question 33. What is justification?

Justification is an act of God's free grace, wherein he pardoneth all our sins, and accepteth us as righteous in his sight, only for the righteousness of Christ imputed to us, and received by faith alone.

Westminster Shorter Catechism

Question 34. What is adoption?

Adoption is an act of God's free grace, whereby we are received into the number, and have a right to all the privileges, of the sons of God.

Westminster Shorter Catechism

Question 35. What is sanctification?

Sanctification is the work of God's

free grace, whereby we are renewed

in the whole man after the image of

God, and are enabled more and

more to die unto sin, and live unto

righteousness.

Westminster Shorter Catechism

Question 36. What are the benefits which in this life do accompany or flow from justification, adoption, and sanctification?

The benefits which in this life do

accompany or flow from justification,

adoption, and sanctification, are,

assurance of God's love, peace of

conscience, joy in the Holy Ghost,

increase of grace, and perseverance

therein to the end.

Westminster Shorter Catechism

Question 37. What benefits do believers receive from Christ at death?

The souls of believers are at their

death made perfect in holiness, and

do immediately pass into glory; and

their bodies, being still united to Christ,

do rest in their graves till the resurrection.

Westminster Shorter Catechism

Question 38. What benefits do believers receive from Christ at the resurrection?

At the resurrection, believers being raised up in glory, shall be openly acknowledged and acquitted in the day of judgment, and made perfectly blessed in the full enjoying of God to all eternity.

Westminster Shorter Catechism

Question 39. What is the duty which God requireth of man?

The duty which God requireth of man, is obedience to his revealed will.

Westminster Shorter Catechism

> Question 40. What did God at first reveal to man for the rule of his obedience?

The rule which God at first revealed

to man for his obedience, was the

moral law.

Westminster Shorter Catechism

Question 41. Wherein is the moral law summarily comprehended?

The moral law is summarily comprehended in the ten commandments.

Westminster Shorter Catechism

Question 42. What is the sum of the ten commandments?

The sum of the ten commandments is,

To love the Lord our God with all our

heart, with all our soul, with all our

strength, and with all our mind; and

our neighbor as ourselves.

Westminster Shorter Catechism

Question 43. What is the preface to the ten commandments?

The preface to the commandments is

in these words, I am the Lord thy

God, which have brought thee out of

the land of Egypt, out of the house

of bondage.

Westminster Shorter Catechism

Question 44. What doth the preface to the ten commandments teach us?

The preface to the ten

commandments teacheth us, That

because God is the Lord, and our

God, and Redeemer, therefore we

are bound to keep all his

commandments.

Westminster Shorter Catechism

Question 45. Which is the first commandment?

The first commandment is, Thou shalt

have no other gods before me.

Westminster Shorter Catechism

Question 46. What is required in the first commandment?

The first commandment requireth us to know and acknowledge God to be the only true God, and our God; and to worship and glorify him accordingly.

Westminster Shorter Catechism

Question 47. What is forbidden in the first commandment?

The first commandment forbiddeth the denying, or not worshipping and glorifying the true God as God, and our God; and the giving of that worship and glory to any other, which is due to him alone.

Westminster Shorter Catechism

Question 48. What are we specially taught by these words, "before me," in the first commandment?

These words, before me, in the first commandment teach us, that God, who seeth all things, taketh notice of, and is much displeased with, the sin of having any other God.

Westminster Shorter Catechism

Question 49. Which is the second commandment?
(Part 1)

The second commandment is, Thou

shalt not make unto thee any graven

image, or any likeness of anything that

is in heaven above, or that is in the

earth beneath, or that is in the water

under the earth: thou shalt not bow

down thy self to them, nor serve them:

Westminster Shorter Catechism

Question 49. Which is the second commandment?
(Part 2)

...for I the Lord thy God am a jealous

God, visiting the iniquity of the fathers

upon the children unto the third and

fourth generation of them that hate

me; and showing mercy unto

thousands of them that love me, and

keep my commandments.

Westminster Shorter Catechism

> **Question 50.** What is required in the second commandment?

The second commandment requireth

the receiving, observing, and keeping

pure and entire, all such religious

worship and ordinances as God hath

appointed in his Word.

Westminster Shorter Catechism

> Question 51. What is forbidden in the second commandment?

The second commandment forbiddeth the worshipping of God by images, or any other way not appointed in his Word.

Westminster Shorter Catechism

Question 52. What are the reasons annexed to the second commandment?

The reasons annexed to the second commandment are, God's sovereignty over us, his propriety in us, and the zeal he hath to his own worship.

Westminster Shorter Catechism

Question 53. Which is the third commandment?

The third commandment is, Thou shalt

not take the name of the Lord thy

God in vain; for the Lord will not hold

him guiltless that taketh his name in

vain.

Westminster Shorter Catechism

Question 54. What is required in the third commandment?

The third commandment requireth the

holy and reverend use of God's

names, titles, attributes, ordinances,

word, and works.

Westminster Shorter Catechism

Question 55. What is forbidden in the third commandment?

The third commandment forbiddeth all profaning or abusing of anything whereby God maketh himself known.

Westminster Shorter Catechism

Question 56. What reason is the annexed to the third commandment?

The reason annexed to the third commandment is, that however the breakers of this commandment may escape punishment from men, yet the Lord our God will not suffer them to escape his righteous judgment.

Westminster Shorter Catechism

Question 57. What is the fourth commandment?
(Part 1)

The fourth commandment is,

Remember the Sabbath day, to keep

it holy. Six days shalt thou labor, and

do all work; but the seventh day

the Sabbath of the Lord thy God; in

it thou shalt not do any work, thou,

nor thy son, nor thy manservant, nor...

Westminster Shorter Catechism

Question 57. Which is the fourth commandment?
(Part 2)

... thy maidservant, nor thy stranger

that is within thy gates. For in six days

the Lord made heaven and earth, the

sea, and all that in them is, and

rested the seventh day: wherefore the

Lord blessed the Sabbath day, and

hallowed it.

Westminster Shorter Catechism

Question 58. What is required in the fourth commandment?

The fourth commandment requireth

the keeping holy to God such set

times as he hath appointed in his

Word; expressly one whole day in

seven, to be a holy Sabbath to

himself.

Westminster Shorter Catechism

Question 59. Which day of the seven hath God appointed to be the weekly Sabbath?

From the beginning of the world to

the resurrection of Christ, God

appointed the seventh day of the

week to be the weekly Sabbath; and

the first day of the week ever since,

to continue to the end of the world,

which is the Christian Sabbath.

Westminster Shorter Catechism

Question 60. How is the Sabbath to be sanctified?

The Sabbath is to be sanctified by a holy resting all that day, even from such employments and recreations as are lawful on other days; and spending the whole time in the public and private exercises of God's worship, except so much as is to be taken up in the works of necessity and mercy.

Westminster Shorter Catechism

Question 61. What is forbidden in the fourth commandment?

The fourth commandment forbiddeth

the omission or careless performance

of the duties required, and the profaning

the day by idleness, or doing that

which is in itself sinful, or by unnecessary

thoughts, words, or works, about our

worldly employments or recreations.

Westminster Shorter Catechism

Question 62. What are the reasons annexed to the fourth commandment?

The reasons annexed to the fourth commandment are, God's allowing us six days of the week for our own employments, his challenging a special propriety in the seventh, his own example, and his blessing the Sabbath day.

Westminster Shorter Catechism

Question 63. Which is the fifth commandment?

The fifth commandment is, Honour thy

father and thy mother; that thy days

may be long upon the land which

the Lord thy God giveth thee.

Westminster Shorter Catechism

Question 64. What is required in the fifth commandment?

The fifth commandment requireth the preserving the honor, and performing the duties, belonging to everyone in their several places and relations, as superiors, inferiors, or equals.

Westminster Shorter Catechism

Question 65. What is forbidden in the fifth commandment?

The fifth commandment forbiddeth the

the neglecting of, or doing anything

against, the honor and duty which

belongeth to everyone in their several

places and relations.

Westminster Shorter Catechism

Question 66. What is the reason annexed to the fifth commandment?

The reason annexed to the fifth commandment is, a promise of long life and prosperity (as far as it shall serve for God's glory and their own good) to all such as keep this commandment.

Westminster Shorter Catechism

Question 67. Which is the sixth commandment?

The sixth commandment is, Thou shalt

not kill.

Westminster Shorter Catechism

Question 68. What is required in the sixth commandment?

The sixth commandment requireth all lawful endeavors to preserve our own life, and the life of others.

Westminster Shorter Catechism

Question 69. What is forbidden in the sixth commandment?

The sixth commandment forbiddeth

the taking away of our own life, or

the life of our neighbor, unjustly, or

whatsoever tendeth thereunto.

Westminster Shorter Catechism

Question 70. Which is the seventh commandment?

The seventh commandment is, Thou

shalt not commit adultery.

Westminster Shorter Catechism

Question 71. What is required in the seventh commandment?

The seventh commandment requireth the preservation of our own and our neighbor's chastity, in heart, speech, and behavior.

Westminster Shorter Catechism

Question 72. What is forbidden in the seventh commandment?

The seventh commandment forbiddeth

all unchaste thoughts, words, and

actions.

Westminster Shorter Catechism

Question 73. Which is the eighth commandment?

The eighth commandment is, Thou shalt not steal.

Westminster Shorter Catechism

Question 74. What is required in the eighth commandment?

The eighth commandment requireth the lawful procuring and furthering the wealth and outward estate of ourselves and others.

Westminster Shorter Catechism

Question 75. What is forbidden in the eighth commandment?

The eighth commandment forbiddeth

whatsoever doth, or may, unjustly

hinder our own, or our neighbor's,

wealth or outward estate.

Westminster Shorter Catechism

Question 76. Which is the ninth commandment?

The ninth commandment is, Thou shalt

not bear false witness against thy

neighbor.

Westminster Shorter Catechism

Question 77. What is required in the ninth commandment?

The ninth commandment requireth the maintaining and promoting of truth between man and man, and of our own neighbor's good name, especially in witness bearing.

Westminster Shorter Catechism

Question 78. What is forbidden in the ninth commandment?

The ninth commandment forbiddeth whatsoever is prejudicial to truth, or injurious to our own, or our neighbor's good name.

Westminster Shorter Catechism

Question 79. Which is the tenth commandment?

The tenth commandment is, Thou shalt

not covet thy neighbor's house, thou

shalt not covet thy neighbor's wife,

nor his manservant, nor his

maidservant, nor his ox, nor his ass,

nor anything that is thy neighbor's.

Westminster Shorter Catechism

Question 80. What is required in the tenth commandment?

The tenth commandment requireth full contentment with our own condition, with a right and charitable frame of spirit toward our neighbor, and all that is his.

Westminster Shorter Catechism

Question 81. What is forbidden in the tenth commandment?

The tenth commandment forbiddeth all discontentment with our own estate, envying or grieving at the good of our neighbor, and all inordinate motions and affections to anything that is his.

Westminster Shorter Catechism

Question 82. Is any man able perfectly to keep the commandments of God?

No mere man, since the fall, is able in this life perfectly to keep the commandments of God, but doth daily break them in thought, word, and deed.

Westminster Shorter Catechism

Question 83. Are all transgressions of the law equally heinous?

Some sins in themselves, and by reason of several aggravations, are more heinous in the sight of God than others.

Westminster Shorter Catechism

Question 84. What doth every sin deserve?

Every sin deserveth God's wrath and curse, both in this life, and that which is to come.

Westminster Shorter Catechism

Question 85. What doth God require of us, that we may escape his wrath and curse, due to us for sin?

To escape the wrath and curse of

God, due to us for sin, God requireth

of us faith in Jesus Christ, repentance

unto life, with the diligent use of all

the outward means whereby Christ

communicateth to us the benefits of

redemption.

Westminster Shorter Catechism

Question 86. What is faith in Jesus Christ?

Faith in Jesus Christ is a saving grace,

whereby we receive and rest upon

him alone for salvation, as he is

offered to us in the gospel.

Westminster Shorter Catechism

Question 87. What is repentance unto life?

Repentance unto life is a saving grace, whereby a sinner, out of a true sense of his sin, and apprehension of the mercy of God in Christ, doth, with grief and hatred of his sin, turn from it unto God, with full purpose of, and endeavor after, new obedience.

Westminster Shorter Catechism

Question 88. What are the outward and ordinary means whereby Christ communicateth to us the benefits of redemption?

The outward and ordinary means whereby Christ communicateth to us the benefits of redemption are, his ordinances, especially the Word, sacraments, and prayer; all which are made effectual to the elect for salvation.

Westminster Shorter Catechism

Question 89. How is the Word made effectual to salvation?

The Spirit of God maketh the reading,

but especially the preaching of the

Word, an effectual means of

convicting and converting sinners, and

of building them up in holiness and

comfort, through faith, unto salvation.

Westminster Shorter Catechism

> Question 90. How is the Word to be read and heard, that it may become effectual to salvation?

That the Word may become effectual

to salvation, we must attend thereunto

with diligence, preparation, and

prayer; receive it with faith and love,

lay it up in our hearts, and practice it

in our lives.

Westminster Shorter Catechism

Question 91. How do the sacraments become effectual means of salvation?

The sacraments become effectual means of salvation, not from any virtue in them, or in him that doth administer them; but only by the blessing of Christ, and the working of his Spirit in them that by faith receive them.

Westminster Shorter Catechism

Question 92. What is a sacrament?

A sacrament is an holy ordinance instituted by Christ; wherin, by sensible signs, Christ, and the benefits of the new covenant, are represented, seated, and applied to believers.

Westminster Shorter Catechism

Question 93. Which are the sacraments of the New Testament?

The sacraments of the New Testament are, Baptism, and the Lord's Supper.

Westminster Shorter Catechism

Question 94. What is Baptism?

Baptism is a sacrament, wherein the

washing with water in the name of the

Father, and of the Son, and of the

Holy Ghost, doth signify and seal our

ingrafting into Christ, and partaking of

the benefits of the covenant of grace,

and our engagement to be the Lord's.

Westminster Shorter Catechism

Question 95. To whom is Baptism to be administered?

Baptism is not to be administered to any that are out of the visible church, till they profess their faith in Christ, and obedience to him; but the infants of such as are members of the visible church are to be baptized.

Westminster Shorter Catechism

Question 96. What is the Lord's Supper?

(Part 1)

The Lord's Supper is a sacrament,

wherein, by giving and receiving

bread and wine, according to Christ's

appointment, his death is showed

forth; and the worthy receivers are...

Westminster Shorter Catechism

Question 96. What is the Lord's Supper?

(Part 2)

... not after a corporal and carnal manner, but by faith, made partakers of his body and blood, with all his benefits, to their spiritual nourshment, and growth in grace.

Westminster Shorter Catechism

Question 97. What is required for the worthy receiving of the Lord's Supper?

It is required of them that would worthily partake of the Lord's Supper, that they examine themselves of their knowledge to discern the Lord's body, of their faith to feed upon him, of their repentance, love, and new obedience; lest, coming unworthily, they eat and drink judgment to themselves.

Westminster Shorter Catechism

> Question 98. What is prayer?

Prayer is an offering up of our desires

unto God, for things agreeable to his

will, in the name of Christ, with

confession of our sins, and thankful

acknowledgement of his mercies.

Westminster Shorter Catechism

Question 99. What rule hath God given for our direction in prayer?

The whole Word of God is of use to direct us in prayer; but the special rule of direction is that form of prayer which Christ taught his disciples, commonly called the Lord's Prayer.

Westminster Shorter Catechism

Question 100. What doth the preface of the Lord's Prayer teach us?

The preface of the Lord's Prayer,

which is, *Our Father which art in*

heaven, teacheth us to draw near to

God with all holy reverence and

confidence, as children to a father,

able and ready to help us; and that

we should pray with and for others.

Westminster Shorter Catechism

Question 101. What do we pray for in the first petition?

In the first petition, which is, *Hallowed be thy name*, we pray, that God would enable us, and others, to glorify him in all that whereby he maketh himself known; and that he would dispose all things to his own glory.

Westminster Shorter Catechism

Question 102. What do we pray for in the second petition?

In the second petition, which is, *Thy kingdom come*, we pray that Satan's kingdom may be destroyed; and that the kingdom of grace may be advanced, ourselves and others brought into it, and kept in it; and that the kingdom of glory may be hastened.

Westminster Shorter Catechism

Question 103. What do we pray for in the third petition?

In the third petition, which is, *Thy will be done in earth, as it is in heaven,* we pray, that God, by his grace, would make us able and willing to know, obey, and submit to his will in all things, as the angels do in heaven.

Westminster Shorter Catechism

Question 104. What do we pray for in the fourth petition?

In the fourth petition, which is, *Give us this day our daily bread*, we pray that of God's free gift we may receive a competent portion of the good things of this life, and enjoy his blessings with them.

Westminster Shorter Catechism

Question 105. What do we pray for in the fifth petition?

In the fifth petitoin, which is, *And forgive us our debts, as we forgive our debtors*, we pray that God, for Christ's sake, would freely pardon all our sins; which we are the rather encouraged to ask, because by his grace we are enabled from the heart to forgive others.

Westminster Shorter Catechism

Question 106. What do we pray for in the sixth petition?

In the sixth petition, which is, *And lead us not into temptation, but deliver us from evil,* we pray, that God would either keep us from being tempted to sin, or support and deliver us when we are tempted.

Westminster Shorter Catechism

Question 107. What doth the conclusion of the Lord's Prayer teach us?

(Part 1)

The conclusion of the Lord's Prayer, which is, *For thine is the kingdom, and the power, and the glory, for ever, Amen.*, teacheth us to take our encouragement in prayer from God only...

Westminster Shorter Catechism

Question 107. What doth the conclusion of the Lord's Prayer teach us?

(Part 2)

… and in our prayers to praise him

ascribing kingdom, power, and glory

to him; and, in testimony of our

desire, and assurance to be heard,

we say, Amen.

Westminster Shorter Catechism

This copywork pack has been created by Amy Maze.

Hi, I'm Amy! I am a homemaker, mother, child of God, blogger, and owner of Classical Copywork. I love to learn, plan, and create. When I am not teaching my children or spending time with my husband, you will find me blogging at Living and Learning at Home and creating new copywork packs like this one!

www.livingandlearningathome.com

www.classicalcopywork.com

Westminster Shorter Catechism

Would you like a free page of copywork sent to your email every week?

Would you like discount codes for copywork packs?

Visit www.classicalcopywork.com and enter your email address to receive one free copywork page and one discount code each week.

As a bonus for subscribing, you will receive the Classical Copywork Sampler!

"Sample pages from each copywork pack at Classical Copywork, packaged together in one convenient download!"

Westminster Shorter Catechism

Did you enjoy this copywork pack?

Then you might enjoy...

www.classicalcopywork.com

www.ingramcontent.com/pod-product-compliance
Lightning Source LLC
Chambersburg PA
CBHW080445110426
42743CB00016B/3283